PROVIDENTIAL

POEMS BY

COLIN CHANNER

Published by Akashic Books
©2015 Colin Channer

ISBN-13: 978-1-61775-405-0
Library of Congress Control Number: 2015934038

All rights reserved
Published in the United Kingdom by Peepal Tree Press Ltd.
First Akashic Books printing

Akashic Books
Twitter: @AkashicBooks
Facebook: AkashicBooks
E-mail: info@akashicbooks.com
Website: www.akashicbooks.com

ALSO BY COLIN CHANNER

Fiction
Girl with the Golden Shoes
Passing Through
Waiting in Vain

Anthologies
Kingston Noir (editor)
*So Much Things to Say: 100 Poets from the First Ten Years of the
Calabash International Literary Festival* (coeditor)
Iron Balloons: Hit Fiction from Jamaica's Calabash Writers Workshop
(editor)

For Charles and Phyllis, the parents

For Addis and Maki, the kids

Acknowledgments

Thanks to the Rhode Island State Council on the Arts (RISCA) for a 2015 Fellowship Merit Award in Poetry, and to the editors of the following publications where some of these poems first appeared: *Prairie Schooner*, *Renaissance Noire*, *The Common* and *Harvard Review*.

I must in addition turn thanks to Kwame Dawes for his steady encouragement, elegant notes and wise counsel. I offer gratitude to Jeremy Poynting of Peepal Tree Press and Johnny Temple of Akashic Books for their stalwart support.

Chris Abani, Olga Broumas, Gregory Pardlo, Chase Twichell, Ishion Hutchinson—from being around you I inhaled much knowing of what it takes to make a poem. Thanks for the secondhand smoke.

Marie Brown has been there since the first book. *The Book of Jamaica* made me want to write.

RISCA
Rhode Island State Council On The Arts
Art is the Anchor

CONTENTS

REVOLUTIONARY TO RASS

(for Perry Henzell)

Rangers.
That is what they are.

Perry shifts in a pink Adirondack
rooted in the grass. We're on a cliff between
a white adobe cottage and the sea.
Canoes crawl far on the red skyline.

In these last years, last months, last days,
he talks like he's always—
grand and sweeping.
The white beard mops his neck.
He plays prophet.

Facing twilight with his son-out-law
relaxing
in the second chair,
the director
who shot Rhygin in a star shirt,
made Cliff reggae Django,
talks like he knows. Still, he proves.

As a boy, and don't forget,
he rode bareback around Caymanas,
prime cane acreage run efficient by his dad.

Yes, man, he'd go riding, boy Perry,
leave the fields, the factory,

the maid-appointed luxury of the busha's lodge,
hair mad like a Hollywood Indian,
track the hill to Pinnacle to scout the Rasta mass,
originals taking refuge in hundreds
homesteading in the pledge of Howell.
Gangunguru Maragh,
vegan, ganjaman, black boss and prophet.
The Gong.

It's not black and white, says Perry,
whiteness warming into ochre—
the sun a setting gel.
It's never been. Look at the sea.
Whether you like it or not—who knows,
you might be into navy, periwinkle more,
I hope—
feelings don't affect a fact.

That water has no color, what you see is an effect,
and, listen, ignore my logic if you want
for I don't business. True is true.

Rangers. That is what they are.
We don't have police here—we have rangers.
Employed by the landful against the landless.
Paid to shoot to kill.

So check it. This whole facking island
is a damn estate, a checkerboard
of traps and schemes. Power game.
What you can expect?

Listen, if I was black like you, Colin.
Well, not like you—you know what I mean—
I'd elect to take up guns.

Ahhhhhhh, Perry.
Revolutionary to rass.

FIRST RECRUITS

They answered when the Queen
called, wanting constables,
dependables,
regulars to keep order after riot
rumbled to rebellion back in 1865,
the year impatience with the free
we'd got came out in uprush.
Thirty years nearly after slavery
and the liberty half cooked.

They're kin to my mother's hill people.
Tea dark. Strong featured.
Hair that gets comb teeth caught up.
Turning on a rush mat, a coir mattress,
lighting a lamp in a tatu cotched
on land with no title,
catching water,
dabbing on a little obeah,
dressing in the fashion
of the humble decent—
careful not to rip, stretch out,
alert for wrinkles,
palming down the seams.

Their minds were rank with the killings
when they went to sign up.
They imagined a hint of burnt wood,
remembered an odour of rot
although History had been clever

with the evidence, had left the dead
outside to menace, later ganged up
scared survivors into throngs,
quick and efficient from habit,
frugal by rote. Not a single finger
more assigned than what backra
thought it ought to take
for wogs to scoop
and chuck and barrow
blood and neighbors into pits.

Of those who came,
nine hundred plus were taken.
Sharp-eyes, big hearts,
plenty meat
between the blades.
Feet with arches.

Walking proudly. Traitors
falling into place.

LEA

I.

They played coc'nut bough
cricket in the growing season,
attended school half time,
otherwise worked with grown-ups,
cutting, ratooning, drawing water
from the spring that drove the wheel.

Thirty years, a generation plus
from slavery, and Lea,
my mother's great-grandad
and Nev, his closest friend,
were living mostly in their
great-grandparents' world,
one of long views to far hills,
but tight boundaries,
force and sense and habit
keeping people in their place.

When militias killed a thousand blacks
out in St. Thomas back in 1865,
put on that famous vigilante pageant
that began with muskets firing
on protesters in a courthouse square,
my mother's great-grandfather was a child.
Still, busha called him for his labor,
told him to get Nev,
made him lead on his pardy,

colin channer / providential

to the lignum vitae woods
to work with grown survivors
heaving corpses into graves.

Imagine that boy, his friend and other children
massed on the bank of a hole,
handling bodies,
lifting, passing, easing down,
the cadence like the one employed
to pack ox carts with hogsheads,
barrels of molasses. Spitting ashes.
Coughing dust.

Now, follow born-free and ex-chattel,
going home at twilight, slow marching,
dressed in rag calico, burlap, osnaburg,
using footbeat to hold a rhythm,
no talking, passing burnt houses,
cottages hit down, then seeing up ahead
odd statues
cast in shadow, set in bush—
no, folks grief struck,
heads down.

Now to this moment add rain.

II.

It's a detail Lea included
when he told the tale
to Phyllis Fay,
his great-grandchild, my mum,

19

who asked about a photo
framed in pewter on a bureau
in the bungalow he lived in
on a farm in St. Ann,
way, way far from St. Thomas,
beyond a watershed,
decent acreage in Gibraltar
hamlet in low hills,
all small holdings,
good people, stone fences,
woods lush with bamboo,
and fat white cows.

It rained for days he told her,
like Bible,
and the whole place smelled of war,
and 'cause everything was broke up
they slept for days in mud
until, thanks be to God, sunshine came back slowly,
and things took time to dry out, and life—
well, it went back to normal,
to duties and habits,
same difference, old usual,
scratching dirt, doing what you do
as 'cording to what season,
planting, reaping—
if busha don't need you—maybe little school.

That's how it was—
you worked as you should,
kept your mind on now,
left behind whatever happened—
as they learned you

with the switch from early—
what to keep, and what to talk.

And so it was. Forgotten.
There, but as a dust of disquiet,
a fog of unease until that first Easter
after martial law when he and Neville,
same Inspector Bledsoe in the photo,
sneaked away to idle,
hunt birds and play cricket in a clearing
near some cedar woods
and corpses started poking from the ground.

From that day,
he told his great-grandchild,
he could see things, cross over and come back,
and that's how he earned a shilling—
selling conference with the dead,
finding well water,
susu-ing what to seed in what season,
when drought would come.

For those he loved
he drew tonics, brewed infusions,
stood as surety for loans,
sat on his porch in Gibraltar,
gave advice in his hat and jacket,
healed with tea and words,
patient with the lines,
sloe eyes blankish,
then took to bed with john crow batty,
crude white rum, sometimes two bottles,
and think and think and think about the killings,

drift to the slaughter
and the what came next,
the digging, the heaving, the
hiding with dirt,
but most of all how quickly
he and Neville took to acting normal,
went back to simple pickney life.

NEVILLE'S LOGIC

He'd been there with the rest
on garbage duty, cleaning up,

chucking bodies into graves,
sweat for eye water,

free born, speaking English,
no clan or tribal language,

no lash markings on the shoulders,
no embossing on the back,

just a skin, a color, a future
with set duties, some roles:

pickininny to whites,
livestock with language,

to blacks—recruit to toughen
up for backra work.

Jamaica? Their country—
Jamaican? Near white

mustee mulatto quadroon

Nation?
Something more than land

colin channer / providential

where you is born,
which busha, which estate,

which district near which town?
Until he sees

courthouse square, St. Thomas,
negro, statue with a breath,

helmet, tunic, face fed
well, no whiskers,

belonging
Jamaica Something Force.

Place, rank and country.
Own it. Pass it on.

CLAN

(for Kwame Dawes)

Every clan has its colors, its history, its foes,
its limits, its ways of notching who's out and in.

Every clan has its parlance, its secrets, its publics,
its fables, its side deals cut with death.

These old street gangs of Kingston,
city ghillies, croton orange, chocho green,

are not manics, but shrewd evaluators
of their worth: shooters part-making an epic,

a story kept in breath, refreshed
at corner fetes of chicken, smoky bread,

at fish spots on the dark foreshore,
waves translating patwa to a lost Aegean tongue.

Hail, Spanglers, Shower,
Byah, Copper, Starkey, Bucky.

Hail, Claudie, Zacky, Rhygin,
Feather Mop.

Every clan has its children, its widows,
its fathers, its prayers, its vengeance pledge,

colin channer / providential

its poems, its dances, its pictures,
its questions never set.

Who gave the order? When will it end?
Every clan has peaks it never gets to,

humps to get over, mounds of buried hurt.
We belongers sieve the fragments

from the midden, make molds.
Shells. Shit. Skin. Seeds. Bone.

MIMIC

I.

From the chopper shot
the beach is a golden border
on a brown-gray shack town,
a jumble on a point,
sweet flourish of Liberia
sweeping into waves.

My son and I are watching
this in lamplight from our low
brown armless couch,
iced roibos on the low wood table
where I keep a bowl of beat-up cricket balls,
a wink to where he indirectly comes from,
Makonnen, Brooklyn teenager
with Antillean roots
replanted in Rhode Island,
a state petiter than the country
where my navel string was cut.

He's a boy who loves sketching,
drawing cartoons, eating fish and pasta,
swimming, but most of all
performing accents, likes how
they jokify the mouth.

He was born with the ears of a mimic,
a tight connect between what makes a sound

colin channer / providential

and how to counterfeit it, make it feel
authentic near its place of birth.

On screen, the camera jerks
behind an ex-warlord
up chipped-up stairs
to a big slab roof.
Here, he's questioned by
a pink and meaty hipster,
dude keen to talk to men
who say they ate their foes in war.

This one here refers
to chopping wide the backs of children,
mimes reaching in the crack
to pluck a heart,
and munching it before a fight
for blood and courage,
naked at times, or done drag,
boots with wigs and dresses,
amulets and other charms,
the more bizarre
the better hidden.
Spirits can evade
the human eye.

Maki echoes all the interviewer's
LA nasals. I laugh hard.
But when he takes on
a Liberian accent
I do not take it well
although I'm twisted
by the sketch, a poly-vocal

back-and-forth involving riots.
It's peacetime and we're at
Monrovia's first McDonald's.
Folks are vexed.
The burgers aren't made
from human flesh.

I gently tell him he,
well, we shouldn't joke too much
about this awful war,
and blah blah on about this country
founded on the coast of Guinea
by ex-chattel,
guide him through the marsh
of history to the present,
leading as a father should a son.

II.

Later, as I pinch out
contact lenses, my own voice
comes blah-blah-ing
from behind the mirror mounted
to the bathroom wall.

I smile at Mr. Silly's talents,
how he switches accents
from Liberian to mine,
hacking vowels,
pitching consonants
precisely in the mouth,
beginning now another improv,

phone calls from police headquarters
in Gbarnga, begging Kingston
for assistance, tips for getting info
out of infants who
despite receiving torture
still refuse to talk.

In my bed, on light cotton,
ceiling fan on slow,
I miscue the iPod in the dock.
Callas, not Lee Perry, comes on.
In my head I talk to Maki
and myself.

The confessors are clan
to killers on an island
I know. Same nose,
same eyes, same trail of razor
bumping on the shine-
clean cheeks. The nicknames
from the news and movies.
Rambo, bin Laden.
The loafers, designer jeans
and polo shirts worn loose.
How they discuss a slaughter
with ease, by rote,
never as something spectacular,
absurd. And I belong to them,
on two sides, for generations,
by blood.

My kinsmen aren't poets.
They're cops.

CIVIL SERVICE

A man-boy of nearly twenty,
slave-dressing in pantaloons
in 1930, slowly reads a *Gleaner*
from behind a stocky "German"
woman in a fabric shop.
Finds himself in love.

Walking home, feet adding shine-ness
to a track cut out of scrub,
he hugs the parcel of organdy
that his mother took on trust,
sounds each word the way he did
at first reading, lips moving,
voice too shy to read inside
his head alone.

Above,
birds form an arrow.

Around,
insects hustle-bustle,
get on with the gnawing,
digging, scraping, the noise-making
of their work.

Ahead,
green mountains gallop
left to right, unbroken herd.

Civil service, says
our young romantic
over and over again.

Maybe where you go
to be *a civilize*
and not *no cunumunu*,
as Miss Lady styled him
when she dressed him down
for reading out her paper,
eye-raping her neck-back.

But it's an error that I live off,
this man-boy's misread,
a blunder he compounded
as he clambered into
walks of guavas, figs
and pomegranates,
fruits with no owner,
taking steeper slopes
toward the ridge his kin
had come to after
getting their free paper,
dug their yam hills,
planted roots.

A better reader
would have gotten
hired by the Royal Mail.

But which colonial system
could afford to waste a fellow
like granddad:

obedient, simple-minded,
burly, color struck.

They couldn't trust him
with an envelope. They
issued him a gun.

OCCUPATION
(for Klive Walker)

When he says he signed up out of Christian duty,
there's a twitch in the lid of his dead glass eye,
a flash perhaps of what had worried him
when independence came in '62.

Working-class, dark, and ambitious,
but scarred in ways he didn't know,
he saw the new country as a Canaan,
land of sweet promise with a flag, an anthem,
and not to be discounted, the ska,
clean pop played by qualified sheet readers,
black men from humble backgrounds
dressed in loafers, ties and suits,
the melodies so near exactly like the jazz
      arrangers borrowed,
the solos rich with Cuban licks,
the very setup so orchestral, seating in rows,
classy negroes, black but modern,
separating us and them—the conga-beating
natives of the world.

He says, once he heard the Rasta drumming
underneath *Oh Carolina* mongrelizing
with the pop he got urgent. Signed up.

The old campaigner finger calls another Appleton,
bites air before the sip, blows out after gulping.
Ahhhhhhhhhh. Fire out and in. Gets quiet.

colin channer / providential

Blinks his good eye plenty, while the dead one
goes adrift as he begins to boast of cordons,
raids, all-out assaults. Pinnacle. Coral Gardens,
Back-O-Wall. Machetes confiscated,
all the caches of illegal books,
and people, strange people, like the dread
who'd rather have his elbow broken than to leggo
        off his ital pot. By then the rum
had soaked his tongue enough to slow it,
change its pace, grace it with cadence
of requiem.

As I leave he says we lost our music
and the country went along. Says Busta shoulda
built a camp until the country bought some boats.
Give them the *Black Star Line!*

Imagine a Jamaica, he says, creaking,
where we still had ska, if not ska then rocksteady,
cover singing, good music, guys in outfits
like Motown, shave clean, looking decent.
Imagine the discipline round here if them damn
reggae rascals didn't overthrow the music
and have Rasta represent Jamaica round the world.
        Cho!

Run for cover, run for cover,
Rebel is taking over, taking over.

FUNERAL

Mimic of seventies westerns and gang epics,
Porter drove up in his rimmed-up
Dodge Avenger, early eighties,
new detective posted
to the station near my house.

Black, plain-speaking angel and a table-tennis hawk,
he spoke justice but believed in fuck-the-courts,
couldn't stomach all the talking, the wigs, the robes,
the downgrading of street knowledge,
the big-up of good argument and proof.

He flew all over Killsome, recompensing,
passing on the message God must not be mocked,
quoting scripture to the beat of a quick trigger finger.
His guard ring from de Laurence steady glowed.

He claimed to be son of an Indian,
a powers man who shot seed from Calcutta
telekinetic, dropped it in Jamaica
in a German shepherd dawg.
Yes, he said, he came out in a litter
far beneath a house, that's why him tricky so,
had super-duper instincts and reflexes
on the station's TT board
where once he won a game against
a corporal
while blindfolded
—and I saw this—
paddling just off sound.

colin channer / providential

At his wake, his tipsy brother
made it known
he was from Portland;
yes, his father was an Indian—
but not from *there*—
just a common coolie man from Clarendon,
and his mother was no dawg, but a puss,
that's why him coulda creep so soft
and gwaan so nice,
then bam bam
man get ketch;

how as a boy he carved a cedar gun,
and practiced pulling it and slapping you
before you moved,
made you call him *Trinity,*
then taunted you
for weeks with, "Trinity is still my name,"
how one time he acted out
The Good, the Bad and the Ugly
word for word, every bloody character and move,
and liked the girls he screwed to call him *Shaft.*

We laughed at the morbid elegy,
the gang of us who made the wake,
and cried, just a bit, not too girlish,
held good the macho at that age
where tears were something left to boys
with hairless crotches—
them and men with pewter chins.

So, one drop per man is what

we rationed,
and each held it to the lid good-good
until his scuffing brought him up
to bless the fastened casket with the myth:
good and evil, guilt and sin.

PORTER'S PRAYER

Whoever whatever
the fuck you are
that keeps me from
rooms where
men hide in cupboards,
that makes me say
my gun is stuck
when sarge gives
me the nod
to end
that boy who traced
our shapes in shots,
who showed me sainthood
in the fraudster
and fear in the mum
who pimped
her one girlchild,
who makes me
pause before a dome
of fruit in a squatters' market
and not
kick the whole thing down,
who makes me know
which whores are men,
which men
horrific to the chicks they love,
whoever the fuck
whatever the fuck
you the thing suspected,

colin channer / providential

you the tickle
you the hint
angel instinct obeah luck,
stalk with me this island,
fix missteps,
watch me as I walk
through screens of ganja blissment,
hiding anger
sudden drops
hot feelings
and dog mess—
mess you skid on easy
in this shitty
on the plain

FLEEINGS

It'll be something to relate in a bar years later,
like when the house he's been blocking
on the ferny hill topside his far hometown is done,
and a small-jawed old fart with fat sideburns
will emerge out of the middle-aged inspector of today.

What he relates won't be like his usuals—
narratives of killings, near misses,
Steve McQueen–like great escapes—
but a quiet retelling of the accident
that made him leave the force to be a poet,
how he stumbled into verse
on this here hot-hot Kingston morning
as he walked across a mess of blood
and wrote in error: *Suspect was advancing,*
not feeling when we opened rapid fire,
stopping him from making good his escape.

INTERMEZZO

She says,
I was whole, uncut, then he.
He slit me, then they.
They heard me, then you.
You took me, then we.
          We talked.

Your questions tease.
Embarrass.
          Strip.

I appeal, sir.
Stop please, don't do this.
Yes, I know him, we are friendly.
But I did not
          give consent.
To him or you.

What now?
Nothing.
What next?

In the future
you will glimpse me
in the market,
in the street.
Think of what you did.
Skin your teeth and call me
bad-word, bad-word, bad-wud
little bitch.

colin channer / providential

Come back
to this station,
reach to the hook
where you hang
your orange peels,
break strips,
make tea.

Me?
Not telling.

Rope way longer
than time.

CLARKEY AND ELMA

colin channer / providential

One chop and the back breaks, a pull-twist
and the sternum gone. It is a rampage,
a fête of blood in the small yard
where the big house chucks a lot of shade.

They watch him work the cutlass,
murmur from the deepness of their rum,
observe the way he holds each chicken—soft,
rubs each one tender with pimento,
talcums it with thyme, spreads each leg
to take the stuffing they enjoy,
that mystery mash of cornmeal, Maggi packets
and green herbs his granny still sends from Troja,
the bottles wrapped in brown paper,
taped up tight-tight in plastic like weed.

They, his squad mates of thirty years,
have come to help him with the work,
a job they've taken on in seriousness
since Elma withered on her bones.

They talk about what they talk about
when they congregate this time of year,
the time itself a place, a henge in a backyard
where the macho is remade into something
more feminine and forceful,
a chapel of easement where they honor
through labor what Elma did alone each year
to celebrate the night their brother broke the water,
mudslid into the world.

They pet the goats and piglets, gain their trust
before the ambush, string them from the almond limb
as Elma used to do in a house frock and water boots,
smoking with the lit end of a Rothmans in her mouth—
still the sidewalk higgler that Clarkey took up.

They kill, they gut, they scald, they skin, they scrape,
and then true butchering begins, the slow unmaking
of the puzzlements God fit together easy,
probing with knife point for surrender,
snapping tendons, uncoupling socket and bone.

Tonight, two hundred will come in congregation
to this flat-roof house to dance and give praise—
inside, on the new cream tiles bribed in from Tampa,
outside, on what's left of the garden
since the last break wall add on.
The girlfriends will come but stay distant.
The wives and their sons will dance.
A televangelist will bless the cake,
and with eyes half open, the men who know
Clarke best, who've seen him spatchcock a chicken
then rub it down tender and right,
will think of Elma's phone calls at all hours,
crying, begging them to come,
trembling how the squaddie flung her to the rug
and pressed a knee between her shoulders
like he thought she might fly,
will remember how they'd rush there,
how she'd sway out as half expected,
half slip hauled up past her nipples,
and Clarke would trudge out, grinning,
chest tatted with bite marks.

Now, as they watch him look with glazed intentions
on the drum pit, they intuit things are different,
so much loss. They approach, nonchalant, encircle.

Breathe.

ON A DRY FIELD IN NOWHERE

(for Ishion Hutchinson)

Barefoot boy
drags left,
wheels right,
head quips and
Vroops!

Chasers skid
then freeze
astonished;
bad-word lips
can't move.

On a dry field
in Nowhere
flash vanish

dust blooming
like a tulip
cupping style
and stigma.

Awed cops pull
and bam-bam
shoot.

Baller beauty
gun salute.

49

BALLS

It's a Magnum in the memory.
Ivory handle. Body silver plate.
I didn't see it, but it's fact, I know.

The boy, though, I saw,
what remained at least,
broken on the hot piazza,
khaki shirt and pants glassy
from the starch pressed in at home.

It was a Wednesday at the stadium,
the only one we had those days,
Tivoli versus Charlie Smith,
Labourites competing with the Socialists,
high school football as rally and picnic,
all those ball tricks known as
salads and *pies*.

Outside, in the oven air,
somewhere between the pink bowl
heaped with cheering
and the sprinter's statue looking like a faucet
you could tap for beer,
the remains of a boy, my age,
head open, brains in splatter,
did just deh-deh,
undignified without the tape or chalking
that embrace a life,
just a broken line of boots

colin channer / providential

around it at slack angles,
tight pants with red striping,
pump-actions carried casual,
muzzles only inches from the waste.

By then the chaos of the killing
had simmered to the normal hustle
of bodies pressing round
the scarecrow turnstiles,
and soldiers in fatigues
taking note with their Stens,
the reek of under-odour,
salty piss and cigarettes,
the hum of syrup drawing bees
to snow cone carts,
the sharp of pepper *swimps* tied in plastic,
baskets of aquariums floating on the head.

The boy was no gangster,
so I gathered from the man who sold me
Shirley biscuits in a pack
and a few loose sticks of gum.
Just a gun bag for an activist
nobody couldn't touch.

"Some o' them a get too bad," he said.
"This one balls get cut."

FIRST KILL

(from a casual conversation with a constable)

Was in Flankers on a Friday night.
Pussy Growler was his name.

Half Chiney chacha boy who got a chance
to go to Cuba as a brigadista.

Came back to MoBay with gun knowledge,
Spanish lingo and a building trade.

Wasn't no gunman, really. Like me,
him was a Libra. Likable.

Man everybody check for. Built a hardware
and a rum bar in the garrison. Gave rebar on trust.

Was a gambler though. Owned a thoroughbred
that couldn't win. Loved a married gal.

Said *ayi yi yi* when my bullet bored
his batty as he fucked, pushed his luck.

The second was my wife.

SECOND SHOT

It felt like a punch.
Tha's all it was,
a t'ump that flung me down.

Then it was light head, and thirsty.
Then envy, of all things.

A kite was caught on a telephone pole.
I wanted to be it, see what it could:
the hills, the sea,
the market where my granny sold guava
and two aunties ortanique,
Crossroads, the triple bill at Carib,
the big bus stop with the bleachers,
the mad man dubbing
on the tower with the clock.

My flesh felt like crepe paper,
bones like bamboo frame,
everything ripped and broken.
Belly trailing blood.

Sawn-off blew me.
I was going and going, and maybe,
I'm thinking,
too far fucking gone.

I wanted height above this Killsome.
Birdview it.

The first shot I got was panic.
The second shot? Plain grudge.

CORPORAL TEEGO BROWN TELLS US WHAT EVERY BARTENDER IN JAMAICA KNOWS

(for Geoffrey Philp)

You need three barmaid,
a thick African,
a slim browning,
but most of all a Indian,
any Indian,
but she have to
work night shift.

TENTATIVE DEFINITIONS

On killing:
Is neither a art
nor a science,
is a job.

On honesty:
A lie for a lie
and a truth for a truth.
Old Babylonian law.

On law:
Say it loud: "Laaaaa."
The sound tell you
say it slack and stretchy.
Hear the punch in "Shot."
Clean.

On death:
From you join
the force is on your marks.
You must be set to go.

FUGUE IN TEN MOVEMENTS

1.

(after a painting glimpsed in Narragansett)

He's standing to his ankles
in rough surf, I think,
shirt flapping, cuffs up.

I squint into the gap
between the novel and the rock.
He's vague, small. Set awkward.

The rock's a squat for seagulls.
Some have lifted, broken off
to arc toward the blue pavilion.
Others soar above the swimmers,
scumbling shit.

When you left your squad
you didn't break, Dad.
You were broken. Plainclothes
washed out.

Is this where you dallied
while we waited?
Dabbler's art fair. South County.
Park near a seawall. Lawn
flecked with white tents.

Is drunk police and wayward father
        not enough cliché?
I mean, bathers, boarders. Really?
        Gulls!

You're too small in this vision,
I can't see the way you're turned.
I'm nearsighted.

Your arms align with the horizon.
Are you lifting? Flying back
to us, your black fluff cluster,
your comfort, your rock, your home?

I see. You're faced waveward.
Your back is to the shore.

2.

The crowd packs up its plastic bowls
of pasta, chips and chicken. SUVs drone
        home.

The off-white sand is stamped with heels
        and elbows,
dots of umbrellas, loops cut by coolers
full of Fiji, Bud and Diet Coke.

I shuffle on, framing with the iPad,
hunching like I used to
with the Hasselblad
I shot with in the eighties,

new migrant mapping old New York,
roaming, plotting new selves,
organizing through the grid,
shooting roundabouts from balconies,
stooping to the flagstone,
the manhole cover, its studs,
eyeing lugs on Doc Martens
propped
on subway benches
punk and daring,
and skin, so much skin:
scars, dimples, razor bumps,
neck rolls, keloids,
stretch marks, tiger print and zebra,
spackle fat.

Toward the water's edge I stumble
on a crate of Heineken, off-kilter
on a mound between the impress
of a lounger and a chaise.

I shoot red stars in close-up, bargain
with matte bottles, thinking
beaded, chilly, definitely,
definitely crisp.

Some lanky girls approach me
glinting, each a *weizen* glass.
Could they have one?
Take 'em.
Do I want one?
No, no . . .

I have tastes. I know patterns.
Seen struggle. Too close.
No, no . . .

3.

It's ten o'clock at night.
I should be leaving.
The lifeguards are gone.
From the rock I hear
the raked Atlantic rustle,
smell an infant algae bloom.

Maki is home cartooning.
Could be swimming at the Y,
planing and replaning water,
rising Junior skimming
with his *chik-chik* beat.

It shames me how my baba labors,
like he doesn't trust my wallet,
like he thinks he's banned forever
from his mother's purse.

My father made no way for me.
Moved. Didn't visit. Died at forty-four.
Had a solid police pension.
Zilch and *nada* were endowed.

"Warm up some tamales,"
I tell Mak-Mak when he phones.
He asks why I keep saying
I'll be home.

4.

Out there, moving north to Narragansett,
a boat implies its presence with its lights.

To the side, around a jut, air glimmers
where a trailer park spreads out.

I hear a mush of fast talk and giggles,
pup barks, sniggers, yuks.

Pop pausing, giving way to old country,
warmblood comfort music riding out at canter,

lead voice cry-breaking, drums recalling reggae,
clopping just behind the beat.

If I were a ghost I'd float into the revel,
wander through that snubbed encampment,

do some good, fix breasts and tickets,
get new tires for trucks, pay debts for meth—

all-in thank-you for improvidence,
for joy shared like winnings from the slots.

Leftish, at some distance, a burly motorcycle
stutter-clutches, rounds a bend, blurts off.

I think I know the song, the strain of it.
I lean my head to filter, pop a contact,

stars go soft one side and I'm half shifted
to my father falling on a curb in Kingston.

Now it's part and also '75,
steam breeze, market sprawling through
its fences to surrounding streets,
harbor ferry sounding as it leaves,
street vendors with bandannas
eating starchy roots and chicken
from enamel, the brick and steel
Victorian terminus
for Metro Cammell trains,
bodies cramming traffic, seeping off
for bargains in back lanes.

And me-him/him-me, now-then/then-now
fore-dreaming in reverse, shifting to the sec
before oncoming coma:

street as whirling sky of chinks,
and splintered bottles, copper filings,
orange seeds and cedar dust and
crystallizing piss.

5.

They say the world is spinning around.
I say the world is upside down.

Same chords like the country.
Joe Higgs. Reggae Argonaut.
Led Bob and them to find the hits,

beleaguered them to buckle
on acoustics in the boneyard,
pull together, fearless
in a ring of white-cap graves.

I could have used a man like that
to lead me on the quest
to find my tender,
teach me that the greatest word is *fail*,
that flaws are clues to patterns,
compassion, bravery's secret name,
and death nothing but a crackle,
the leaving of a shell, a lifting into legend.
Flight.

6.

I don't have the ken for constellations.
My son Makonnen—he's fabulous at that.
Can point out Pisces, Hydra, Cetus.
      Easy.
See each graphic printed out.

His stargazing looks like blessing.
Pointer dotting every twinkle
as a priest would bless
a blemish on a mule,
a lamb, a ferret,
all creatures,
small and big.

He tends to look beyond specifics
into archetypes, has gotten
some instructors worked up.

He was born to be a bigwig
in a pagan order, so I've teased him.

In cave days he was the *dude*,
that one who saw herds
in the dense night lights,
and night lights mimicked
in the pocked rock walls,
and mixed up blood and pigment
to graffiti on this point
and got pissed because he had
no grunt for *imperfect* or *perspective*,
or tools to rub his clumsy pictures off,
the anguishing mythmaker
we echo, and echo, and echo today.

7.

The blips are lisping way below the line
where stars begin to gush.

I peer beyond blank sand
and formless ocean to the winks,

testing limits, hunting shapes and wavers,
blotches edging into silhouette.

I lack the eyesight of the mariner,
the clarity, the length,

the sweeping range from center
off to edge.

But I share the sailor's knack for patterns,
his flair for using shards and chunks

to see entire spheres.
I never apprenticed. Taught myself,

for I was dropped and broken early,
not touched up so I fudged up

snot and tears for glue, hence my patterns:
fuck up, get up, fix up, then go swashing

back to quest for love, leaving her a shambles.
Wrecker and the wreck.

8.

Kingston 1955
(for my mother)

You sit beside your husband
in the Dettol-smelling ward.
Half listen while he slurs
in dream fever. Hatted nurses
drowse about.

Same damn arm closed up
and opened half a dozen times

and still stiff, but stiff now
with a shift in color,
hue change and—*Oh rass!*—goo trickle,
worst of all a faint unfurling
of a graphic odour, almonds,
signal that a limb must be removed.

Through the window, trees
and roofs are getting graced
by bird shadow. Streets repeat
the sign of the cross.
But you see none of this
for what it is to optimists.

You, pragmatic girl who came to town
to be a druggist, are no longer
in this now, but off reckoning
with Big Master in a concocted tense,
the *certain future possible*,
the *what must be*,
imagining a face, hearing a voice,
English with a local tingeing—Golding,
orthopedic legend of the polio epidemic
and Her Maj's royal army corps.

Weeks later, while the frigger
heals from Golding's genius,
you, a twenty-something version of my mother,
feed my sister from a bottle
while obsessing on the bitch
who winged your husband,
begrudging, wanting the wanton's life.
Not all of it. A spec of it.

The sec she latched on good
and got the married liard—jooking,
then jerking to uncatch her pick from bone.

Still, at weird moments, say before
you funnel bulk emulsion into vials,
you'll catch yourself reflecting
on the times you see the retrofitted fucker
nurse Claudette, your infant,
how he sets his bad hand on the table,
pulls each budded finger to conform
a grip around the ribbed warm bottle.
How he drizzles in the creamy O-Lac
with his left hand like a native,
blabba-dabbing with the baby
like a bloody idiot when he's
back to being a cop.
And every time you think of this
a tremor triggers in your womb.

But at night you tug o' war with anger,
fret on ethics, think of *how*,
plot in that concocted tense of yours—
the *certain future possible*,
imagine making traceless toxins,
choking bitches long distance.
No prison! No proof!
        —but always, always,
this dark vision disappears
when you hear your husband's sleeve in rustle,
right arm self-exhuming,
right hand resurrecting warm and vimful
from linen
        —in your dreams at least.

As louvres frill salt wind
across your silver nightie,
you turn inside yourself as long fingers
take the measure of your body,
its curves,
and it's love as it was,
or might have been—you double think—
when you first moved in
to settle in that one room start-up
off the back porch of that old green house
just up from Bournemouth Gardens
where in courting days
your husband used to make a W
with his arms across your scapulas
and waltz you back and forth
and round and round to Cuban ballads
on the deck beside the sea,
your dark skin lit with prickles,
night of bright stars.

9.

I can't decipher constellations.
Moon is all I know.
It is simple, pictographic,
the shield, the wreath, the clock.

From this beach here in South County
I see all of them as smudges
next to or behind the
silver wedge.

Sky,
I'm shouting out to you.
Goddammit!
Reveal a fucking mystery.
Show me something.
Reorganize yourself.
Turn simple.
I'm here for answers on this
fortieth anniversary
of the day my father tried to die.

Not when he died completely,
when he fell that time he came to town to
find his children after years and years
of living in his country district,
drinking with his brethren southpaw.

I went there once, where I think it happened.
Walked along the dirty there near Darling Street,
a sooty place of noise and garbage,
porticos collapsing, zinc roofs downed in rust.

Gulls from Kingston Harbour dove in
now and then to pick at pigeons over *scrapses*.
White *cantankerizing* gray.

It harrowed me to wander round
the places where he staggered
off a bus to get some coins from old friends,
in case he saw his children.

The sidewalk was uneven.
I think he might have been attempting to be sober.

Maybe needed two more drinks,
but then his breath, his smell.
Perhaps getting drunker
would have helped him straighten out.

I saw him, nervous, tired, jonesing for rum.
Walking how he used to on patrol,
pausing midstride or he would topple,
arms out in case he lost all balance,
riding out a thermal. Hurt bird.

He was standing in the street one-legged
when the bus came round the corner
leaning, market baskets piled up on its roof.
There was swerving, braking, shouts,
a weave and then a wiggle
just before the mirror kissed him,
spun him, spun him,
sent him twisting in wobble to the curb
where he froze off his kilter,
arms creaking, trying to rise,
eyes rehearsing coma,
sidewalk spinning up to him,
insides turning over,
world of upside down.

10.

Sky, be honest,
the cops who washed
round the bend
in their Zodiac,

the dolts who thought him dead,
did they chalk him,
give him outline,
in the grit?

If I keep staring
will you make a shape for me,
a constellation?

Gull with Broken Wing.

Coda
(note to self for son)

Giggle.
See the joke in spillage.
Elevate the silly.
Exalt the small.

Allow the wind its rampage.

Assume—but only grandly.
Speak like *bravo* and *gusto*
are words in your tongue.

August is waning,
Days will lose flavor.
Pepper will be lost.

KIK-KIK, PAK-PAK

The back porch is where
her father used to sit on Sundays
after church to clean his gun.
She would sit on the step below him
in her long skirt and beret
typing what he called her foolishness:
letters to the editor, plays about domestics
and dialectic, poems she imagined
Lennon turning into songs.

One day there was a jamming
in her Smith Corona,
and in trying to fix it
she just made it worse.

Her father left his Smith & Wesson
on the gray Formica table
that they used to eat on in the years
before he got promoted.
He spread a sheet of newsprint
on the blue and orange tiles,
divided her tool into parts.

Like most things,
he did this operation in silence,
pointing every now and then
to teach by example.
She began to mimic.
Miming led to picking up:
cylinders, rods, hammers, gears.

He returned to his own assembly.
She resumed her vocation with words.
Kik-kik-kik, steel percussing.
                    Dirty words.
She took her smooth contraption
off her lap, looked across her shoulder,
watched him spin the barrel,
spin the barrel, lock it,
flash it open, look for bullets,
slap it, lock it, cock the hammer,
pull the trigger,
pak-pak-pak-pak-pak, and pak,
smiling at the pitch of it,
locksmith hearing tumblers sing in key.

GENERAL ECHO IS DEAD

(for Muma Nancy)

and no one knows.
Big John dropped.
Fluxy silenced.
No more Echo Tone.

The three bodies heaped
together make a warped, wet star,
limbs flopped and sogging,
a mess of ugly, a surprise
entangled in a net
dragged by police.

General Echo is dead
and no one knows.
Big John dropped.
Fluxy silenced.
No more Echo Tone.

The effectives stand around
smoking, rowdy, bearded,
nothing uniform to them.
They smile and point
at the hump of wet flesh
like it's a plane shot down
and splattered,
owning the execution
in the way of guerrillas
fighting a state when they're the badged and badgers.
Sten guns hang to the gut—IDs.

General Echo is dead
and no one knows.
Big John dropped.
Fluxy silenced.
No more Echo Tone.

A picky-hair boy trots out
ash-ankled, dutty nappy undone,
belly puffing as he slobs
a spoiled banana like a trumpet
ringing the alarm.

ADVANTAGE

Not avoiding the question, Channer.
Lemme done this Guinness Stout.
So round '72, at Half Way Tree,
while doing night duty, a pregnant girl come in,
girl of say twenty, looking haggard,
have on nothing but a pink half slip
pull to her bosom like a baby-doll dress,
and she and the material frowsy,
coc'nut oil, sweat, piss and man cologne
mix with smoke and camphor.

Ordinary, batter-foot girl, no shoes, barefooted,
toe-them spread like fingers, calf-them thick,
so right away I know she come from country—
and her thigh them nice and fat.

She holding her head and bawling,
just bawling and plaiting back her hair
which was an aggravated frazzle,
patches ripped out from the root.

But what hold me, what move me,
was what was running down her legs,
a mix of blood and substance,
pink, see-through, and red.

Gunman broke into her house in Kencot
while she sleeping, she tell me.

colin channer / providential

She just hear a sound, jump up,
strike a matches to light her lamp
and see a shadow by her bed,
and a man begin to take advantage.
Gun on her temple, something rugged
like a saw 'gainst her ribs
and she beg him, "Do sah, you no feel
me belly how me pregnant. Do sah.
Beg you. Do."

So the man finish him thing now, Channer—
and she was plain in her language with this—
him ease off, stand up, zip up, fart,
feel him way to her little folding table,
feeling, for the place still dark,
and all she hearing is pick up and put down,
clink and clunk, wondering what him want,
and then him stop. Guess what?
Him find a tin o' bully beef, must be
the shape make him know, or the key,
and him bright and beg her cook it
with some ketchup, give him
bully beef, ketchup and white rice.

Woman and man different, you know, Channer.
Them make different from we in truth.

Listen, she say when she start to cook
she get a joyful feeling, for the baby
really start to move, and every kick and t'ump
she just take it as life, and where there's life
there's hope.

She lean 'gainst the wall and listen him eat.
Hear him burp. She tell him "Welcome"
when him thank her, then say "Savior!"
when she feel a second pressure from the gun.

So me ask her which way him turn.
If when the stove was on she get a glimpse.

She say she can't answer no question,
for her brain tired, say I must go see for myself,
because the man advantage her so much
the second time him drop asleep.

I didn't even bother wake him up.

SKETCH: A TRIPTYCH

(for Gregory Pardlo)

1: *Duet*

You edit: *Yes a moustache.*
He shades until you nod: *The lip is filled.*

Facts are facts.
You smelled him mostly,
his pencil line an odour
reek of kiss.

In this office,
gazed on by bright portraits,
your detective's other work,
you draw up on your woman's tool,
hoodoo, certain instinct,
mask as you did in the roughing,
catch your attacker in essence,
summon him by the sketching:
Tchick, tchick, tchick tchick, tchick.

2: *Pantomime*
(from *Journal of a West Indian Proprietor* by Matthew Lewis, 1816)

This morning my picture was drawn by a self-taught genius, a negro
Apelles, belonging to Dr. Pope, the minister; and the picture was
exactly such as a self-taught genius might be expected to produce.
It was a hard straight outline, without shade or perspective; the hair
was a very large black patch, and the face covered with a uniform

layer of flesh-color, with a red spot in the center of each cheek. As to likeness, there was not even an attempt to take any. But still, such as they were, there were eyes, nose, and mouth, to be sure. A long red nose supplied the place of my own snub; an enormous pair of whiskers stretched themselves to the very corner of my mouth; and in place of three hairs and a half, the painter, in the superabundance of his generosity, bestowed upon me a pair of eyebrows more bushy than Dr. Johnson's, and which, being formed in an exact semicircle, made the eyes beneath them stare with an expression of the utmost astonishment. The negroes, however, are in the highest admiration of the painter's skill . . .

3: *slowconsciouslikeoblivious*

It's all assured below us,
dark thick wood dance floor;
dry night in cold Foreign,
ginger hipster spinning
scratchy reggae tunes.

We know the songs—this is ritual and revel,
so we listen for the what-a-come,
the when-the-singer-hitches,
the snare rim clap
that shocks us to that inner stillness
while our limbs remain kinetic
as the all-but-the-bass falls out.

We welcome this drop toward absence,
this sheer-off to that Coney Island starship
where the round room whips until
the disco flooring gives

and we get kicks from the flight-like,
backs wall-stuck by force
so different from the one that snatched us up.

In the dub, when the beat breaks down,
we get giddy, sense gray water then get real cool,
move in slowconsciouslikeoblivious,
vigilant for the *chekeh*
shiv of the Gibson,
pointer of the way back to home.

KNOWING WE'LL BE MOSTLY WRONG

We never had a meal alone ever, alone, just us.
We might have, but the memory is gone.
When I see you eating we're never there,
me, Gary or Mum.

It's always you and Claudette.
It's always late, quiet, no buses.
Every now and then a motorbike
muttering up the road.

The rest of us have eaten, done homework,
traveled the planet once again through Viewmasters,
tonged puppy doodoo from the garden,
watered the common hibiscus and crotons,
washed our feet and gone to bed.

The food has been fridged. Fricassee chicken,
or stew beef with carrots, or pig trotters
with broad beans, or macaroni with mince.

You're too drunk to take what's been set apart for you,
to negotiate each thing without over-knocking bottles,
to prime the stove, light each burner,
set the knobs correctly
for the blue beneath the pot.
              Yes, somewhere in some other country
there were microwaves and frozen courses
for drunk husbands,
but when your outside woman didn't feed you
you were left out on your own.

You and Claudette are pulling at the quilty bread
you've brought under your arm,
smearing the off-white with pink bully beef,
Libby's or Grace's, smutted with tan fat and bronze jelly.
          She's twelve and already plumping
from eating two dinners, already using nighties
and dusters and house frocks to fog her shape.
Your knee is unsteady when she sits.
You know you can't ask her to ease up.
You kiss her cheek, hand-feed her,
let her bring the raw scotch bonnet
to your moustache, line it up for you to crunch it
while she pinches at the stalk.

My son, who's ten years older than I was
when I last saw you, will soon leave for school,
a downhill walk from the heights of Providence,
downtown through its sad reaching for recovery,
across an interstate that mainlines to Boston.
He goes to Classical High.

It's the last day of the term.
I am up before him as always,
and not because I am good,
but because he needs direction,
          watching,
coaching step by step into the sweet how
of simple things, like getting up and getting dressed,
keeping track of time, checking off reminders—
the small bits of habit that if multiplied
can bring him bounty.

He's sixteen, but young, tenderhearted,
and has just one friend, a good one,
has never tried Facebook, doesn't see the need to tweet,
makes elaborate illustrations in Moleskin only,
and takes his medication now without embarrassment,
no longer uses their official name, just *the pills*,
which make him feel the way he does
after a hard lap swim—
      relaxed, even and balanced,
not like he's about to drown from all this everything,
or walk on water fire
just to dazzle everybody with his light.

At his age you were farming.
In that red-ground district that's all there was to do,
spade and hoe and scatter corn to gray pigs
and hand off seeds to the wind to do the rest,
make rough note of which black goats which boy
was herding down which trail toward which common—
which shirtless boy I should have said,
because all boys in red-ground districts
then were shirtless and walked
on flat ground with bent knees
from the practice of rolling with the hills,
had toes spread wide like fingers,
and were short for their age.

Your grandson is tall,
slender in the way of his mother and her ilk,
but not petty and vindictive. Open and forgiving—
like you—of other people, but also of himself,
which can be its own concern.

This morning, over sugared coffee
concentrated in a German press,
I gazed at my son from one end
of a short table covered with a cloth
decorated with yellow zigzags—
something I picked up from an outlet.
The wood is good, Italian,
and he still spills milk and juice.

        On this, his last day of school,
he is happy, not because school is ending
but because he is midway into a season
of waking up and going to bed with no reason
to consider not wanting more life.

As I look at him, thinking of the cape of sad
he drew around him when he moved here
in the new year of an awful winter,
he asks why I'd been laughing in my room.

I feel put upon.
I wasn't even aware I'd been laughing,
and then I remember, but it's about one of those things
you find funny for reasons you can't explain,
so I keep saying, oh it's nothing,
and he keeps asking,
and I want him to leave me alone
and go back to feeling lonely
and just go to school. Live his own damned life.
Then I remember you and your daughter,
my sister, at a table sharing time
and something simple for the stomach,
and imagine with the clarity of middle age
how those nights when you came home drunk

and she'd waited up for you,
times I might have glimpsed
while going to the bathroom after wetting the bed,
times it was just the two of you
at the gray and white Formica table
with the green creeper reaching
out and over the clear glass bowl,
the holster slung over a chair,
the brown horse neck of the black revolver,
all of this lit soft by accident,
because low watts were all we could afford;
the air outside fuzzy with warm dampness
and the furry atmospherics of dry leaves,
stirred by mice, mongooses and insomniac bugs,
were perhaps the last things she thought of
that evening a few years ago
when her heart stuttered on her way home
from working at a halfway house in Pittsburgh,
where she taught men who'd done time,
time and time again, what it meant,
what it felt like, or could, to have a simple meal,
in humble light, with a person who had failed
and would fail again.

This morning, as my son leaves for school
in his turquoise polo shirt and gray drawstrings,
hair mown and edged off,
he thanks me for the waffles and the coffee,
and for taking the time to explain the joke.
It is clear from his face he doesn't get it,
that it's so personal it can't be explained.

Perhaps I failed at the telling,
but he is smiling—for the time at the table,
and maybe for the light spreading
on the meadow he was off to enter—
unaware of all the ways I have already
let him down, aware, too, of some ways
I'm not tuned into, so can't mention,
but I know the list is long,
but I also know he's loving,
is likely to be gracious in assessment—I hope—
this boy who was manhandled
out of anger, written off
and given up on,
in the end abandoned,
the exile different from yours
in execution, but still a cut,
a wound, a wound familiar to me,
to us, Gary, Claudette, that fat girl
in the house frock
who'd always wait for you,
who died riding in an ambulance,
alone.

We begin to fail the second we invest in the speck
that makes the children. We do right,
knowing we'll be mostly wrong.

PROVIDENTIAL

1.

Rainstorm in Providence.
End of summer. Good one too.
Afternoons of hot sand,
cold roibos, couscous with nuts,
and gazpacho. Chatty rides
to South County in the gray Passat,
me and my son, reggae puffing in the doors.

1-95 to Route 1, then a cottage lane
that stammers into dirt.
East Beach. Our favorite.
Plain white beauty with a broad lagoon behind.
Three miles and no clubhouse
like Wheeler or Misquamicut,
just warm-tinged alabaster,
a few cream chairs for lifeguards
and wild water—
the West Indies if you add some palms,
sea grapes, lean lunch counters
and music, music, music
played loud, loud, loud.

Fall soon come.
A season I grew up calling autumn.
With it will come pippins, galas,
veggies with dark foliage,
heartbreak with the Knicks,

a birthday if I make it—fifty—and
more rain, more damp,
damp air and more drizzle.

In this house, on this couch,
in this half darkness,
the water gossips of New England's bastard past,
how volcanic islands made it with Laurentia,
got soil and magma nastied up,
how glaciers roughed and cut this new formation,
left behind some payment for the hurt:
lakes, ponds and harbors, rivers for the mills.

Jamaica, where I come from,
is a mostly coral island,
a rough-made sediment bed.
Still, it feels volcanic,
eruptive in the way of newish nations
built on old foundations of violence,
geographies where genocide and massacre
hang like smoke from coal fires,
mosquito nets. There but not there.
Always there but never present.
Where modern murder is considered different
from the older kind,
the kind enacted by Brits in red jackets,
dunce militias put together by Creoles,
before a new black order.
1860s: full-time paid police.

By dint of blood I belong
to this paramilitary,
am clan to it,
lake, to river, to sea.

colin channer / providential

2.

Water misting windows, silvering the glass,
heel-space nudged on the long bench table
set with notions in half shadow—
mail, some novels, a domino tin,
tea mugs, tweezers,
DVDs below a bowl of bruised-up cricket balls,
the printout of a note to handwrite
to Addis, my daughter,
first-year college girl in Vermont,
among trees in orange hats
and bronze earrings.

By Thanksgiving
they'll be nude
and she'll be here
for the chatter and partaking,
but not in this flat.
At a restaurant, the four of us,
father, brother, girl and mum.
Inconvenient and stupid.
A matter of law.

Is this what it's all about,
children and Thanksgiving?
The past is seeping in because of this?

Or is it 'cause I'm turning fifty,
and foggy 'bout the mathematics,
the axes of the graph,
the x and y of the short equation,
the length and angle of the plotted line.

Or could it be this second glass
of Chardonnay. Dry, unoaky,
with a mineral linger,
assertive, bold,
so unlike this tepid feeling
flaking on my joints, crusting my bones,
a sentiment not unlike nostalgia
in its color, but reminiscent of sorrow
in its tone.

It doesn't always come with rain,
this unnamed feeling,
doesn't always come when summer ends
and maples start rehearsing their dress-up,
or each time I look ahead to holidays,
anticipating hissed responses re the children.

I like autumn, the rituals of harvest,
the cool nights, the multiplex of smart movies,
lights whirling over midways,
hog races, pumpkins bigger than cows.

The tepid feeling comes at times,
some times, times when I think
of certain places. This much I know.

Addresses, phone numbers,
a face that brings aromas
of old habits, desires, and haunts,
reflections on how I end up moving
when I think, okay I'm settled.
Wellesley, Brooklyn,

Jersey (two towns), exurbian Atlanta,
the Bronx and Kingston,
frigging Kingston, place of birthright,
accent and language,
disappointer who knows
what bland and what pepper will please.
When I'm with you God understands me
when I laugh in anguish,
where I stole early, and continued,
books and magazines mostly,
every now and then pet fish
and foreign gum,
and gambled, Crown & Anchor,
and the horses.

        Channerebel. Drunk policeman's
bad pickney. The poet. The liyad.
The brainiac. The immature class outlaw.

3.

From another room, low music,
a montage of it—iTunes on shuffle.
Shuggy Otis warbling down
and mushing to Cise Evora, *morna*,
sound of another slave island,
São Vicente, Capo Verde,
a rock in a necklace broken off
the Guinea Coast.

Is this what I'm feeling, *saudade?*
Can that yearning even live outside
its language? Is it portable, translatable,
universal like *the blues?*

The rain eases; Junior Murvin
fades up all breezy,
his reggae bassless at this volume,
just a tinny-tink of drums.

Police and thieves in the streets,
Fighting the nation with their
guns and ammunition . . .

            The guitar phasing,
bending like a saw,
            sends vibrations in the higher heights
smoked of by Lee Perry,
            Scratch,
                        the producer,
                                    itinerant prophet
            of the ghetto psychedelic,

now Satchmo, Queen,
 floaty Joe Harriot,
Abba, Fela,
 Madeleine Peyroux, then Black Uhuru.
General Penitentiary.
 So much bass to the heavy
 the speakers buzz.

The lyrics keen, insist as memories must
in *olvidado*'s shadow. Etch.
The hold. The cell. The pen.
Voice flaking suffering
for the smell indicts all ovens.
The dark. The time. The door.
Then,

When the morning come, I & I would run to get some tea,
but here comes the bosuns with their batons . . .

I put the glass down, sit cross-legged,
eyes closed, inhaling deeply,
suddenly anxious,
caught up in a sudden flood
of requiem, holding to the self
while being moved along,
carried by the river in a give-and-take
that reggae has no name for
the way the *morna* has *el saudade*,
but which the Wailers
heard in the whip snap
of breadmen steering carts
of succor pulled by mules.

I remember on the slave ship
how they brutalize our very soul . . .

And I'm feeling this while hearing Black Uhuru
and it's like I'm taking flight above Kingston,
skimming the Wareika mountains,
shooting up, up, up in hot wet air
over ruffling rusty roofs,
rippling under palms and mango branches,
the street vendor's blue tarp,
now out, out for miles,
crossing the wide gray harbor,
now wheeling back to make smoke signals
where Selassie's DC-9 appeared in '66,
breaking through the rain clouds,
gleaming silver cross,
then turning tightly, sweetly, arms out,
to come in low, low and cautious,
my back to the west and the big red gantries
bearing east to where the jetties used to be,
and there reigns the penitentiary,
superstructure with gun turrets
on the old slave port,
exposed in myth lighting as
a multimasted clipper run aground.
Broken but still useful.
Still crewed with bosuns—
men who drive other men as work.

4.

The return to Providence is easy,
eye-opening. Nothing has changed.
It is still raining in New England
where the clipper left from,
heading south, down along the coast,
then into open water to the Antilles
for sugar, molasses and rum,
hulls low-sitting on the outward journey,
full of dried cod for building strength
in slave labor, efficient salt and protein,
fuel bought and sold in bulk.

Bedtime. A tie-dye onesie
and a hot thermos in a sweater trim
for extra heat below the red Korean mink.
No more music. Just NPR muttering
in a British accent, rain,
the odd car engine and breath.

I'm still fixed on the bosun,
the drover, the prison, the ship,
the clear relations, brazen patterns
in those tall thick walls,
those old redbricks,
still drowsing in wine and *saudade*
and the feeling named by Bob.

It's not lost on me;
I don't indict New England.
I grieve when it's grieving.
Cheer for its teams.

Try to find the flavor
in its bland cuisine,
yet I can't let off the bosun,
the babylon, Jamaican police.

No reconciliation
even in this prelude to harvest,
to forgiveness, bounty and love,
to gratefulness and prayer,
to leaves in good cheer
when the woods will get brazen,
extroverting like it's possible
to remain shining at the height of color,
that radiance will be theirs for life,
like it's rumor, they're destined to lose it,
to go to blank in slow dissolve,
that leaf-by-leaf they'll fall
into their own bereavement,
till spring.

5.

So,
bosun, Babylon, beast,
ticks, lice, corpie, blue stripe,
red seam, DC, blue bag, speshy,
you are my father and grandfather,
are my neighbors growing up.

Mr. Walker who weighed
three hundred pounds
and so was nicknamed *Cannon*.

Mr. Morgan who was shot
one morning after dropping
his missus to the haberdashery.
Took a quick stop to get some feed
for his chickens and *bam,*
a man he'd collared years before
caught him with arms full
and off balance with a foot
on the Austin's short
running board.

Mr. Hunt, too light-skinned
to say good morning.

Mr. Forrest, so rigid he obeyed
a red light in Liguanea
at two in the morning, tempting robbery,
which found him quite attractive
and came. Three in the body
and two to the face,

but didn't kill him yet.
That tuffian drove his green Cortina
down Hope Road, hit a tree
and died alone, no last laugh
for the wicked.

Brickhead, soccer ref with knock knees
who let games flow nice and open
down at Maverley, a field of gray dust.
Tweeted only for outlandish fouls.
Cool all around. But panicked
while on duty at the stadium.
Mini-riot, oranges flung,
yes, some at him,
then beer bottles. Jesus Christian
the Remington shot.
Many hurt, his one job lost.

Porter, country boy like Ivan
in *The Harder They Come*,
just wanted stardom,
couldn't sing so he acted out
his own procedurals, action dramas,
copycatting what he saw at Carib.
Jazzed in boss clothes
and mafia glasses
as he went about the biz
of cleaning things up.

Berry, auxiliary,
just a speshy,
part-time police. Muscle-tight bully
with a badass Chevelle
who used his own gun,

not the short-nose .38 of standard issue
but a Magnum .44.
Ruger, chrome of course,
imitating not the screen
but Man Joyce, his cross-dressing
macho mother who lashed her leg
with a holster and died of what I can't recall,
but sometime before her son was tried
for murder, his girlfriend
a soft target, nothing like his mum.
Berry, what's your number?
What's it like there at GP,
down there off Elletson,
catty-corner from the depot
where my father went for training
in the fifties after coming from the country
up to Bible school and being converted
by his brother Victor who informed him
that he had the height
to get some boots
and start out solid,
and that pastors
got no income
till they got a church?

I am toasting all of you
and none of you,
cussing every one of you.
One day you'll be disowned.

It's raining in Providence.
Autumn soon come.
Next, winter.
        Till the starlings sing out.